Eight Lights for Eight Nights

A Hanukkah Story and Activity Book

Story by Debbie Herman
Activities and Illustrations by Ann D. Koffsky

BARRON'S

For my brother, Mike, a.k.a. Word Boy.
—D.H.

For my boys, Aaron, Jeremy, and Mark, too.
—A.K.

Acknowledgments

The Authors wish to thank the following people: David Becker, Sheri Feld, Alison Fixler, Alan Gersch, Charlotte Herman, Michael Herman, Elizabeth Lazaroff, Rebecca Nenner, Rebecca Rimer

All inquiries should be addressed to:
Barron's Educational Series, Inc.
250 Wireless Boulevard
Hauppauge, New York 11788
http://www.barronseduc.com

International Standard Book No. 0-7641-2600-8

Library of Congress Catalog Card No. 2003049554

Library of Congress Cataloging-in-Publication Data
Herman, Debbie
    Eight Lights for Eight Nights / Debbie Herman and Ann D. Koffsky.
        p. cm. — (Holiday book series)
    ISBN 0-7641-2600-8
        1. Hanukkah—Juvenile literature.   2. Jewish crafts—Juvenile
    literature.   3. Handicraft—Juvenile literature.   I. Koffsky, Ann D.
    II. Title.   III. Series.

BM695.H3H47   2003
296.4'35—dc21   2003049554

Printed in Hong Kong
9 8 7 6 5 4 3 2 1

Contents

The holiday of Hanukkah is a time of great happiness. It is celebrated for eight days, beginning on the 25th day of the Hebrew month of Kislev. This falls in the winter—usually in the month of December. But why do we celebrate Hanukkah? It is all because of a story that happened over 2000 years ago, in the land of Judea, part of present-day Israel. Here's how it goes.

The land of Judea came alive in the early morning sun. Children raced among its hills. Shepherds herded their sheep, farmers tilled the soil, and olive pressers, with huge stone wheels, pressed olives into oil.

And on a mountaintop, in the city of Jerusalem, stood the holy Temple, where the Jewish people came to worship God. There was music and singing, and joy filled the air.

But peaceful times would soon end.

One day, just as the people of Jerusalem were starting their morning, they heard angry shouts, and the rumble of galloping horses. The noises grew louder and louder.

"What's going on?" the people asked each other, as they gathered outside their homes.

A man on horseback galloped their way. He was wearing heavy armor, and waving a shiny sword.

"I am an officer in the mighty Syrian army!" he roared. "And we have just captured your little country! Judea now belongs to King Antiochus the Fourth, and you Jews belong to him too!" The soldier laughed a wicked laugh and galloped off.

Soon after, Antiochus' soldiers stormed through Judea, destroying everything in their paths. They charged into the holy Temple, stealing its gold and silver vessels, erecting statues of their gods and sacrificing swine on the holy altar.

But that was just the beginning.

FUN FACTS

Antiochus called himself Antiochus *Epiphanes,* meaning "I am a god," but because of his excessive cruelty to the Jews and his many bizarre behaviors, people called him Antiochus *Epimanes,* meaning "Antiochus the madman."

Those Jews that adopted the Greek customs were known as Hellenists.

A famous story is told about a woman named Hannah, who had seven sons. Hannah had raised her sons to be so strong in their Jewish beliefs, that when given a choice to worship an idol or die, they chose death.

Antiochus was Greek, and he wanted everyone in his kingdom to act, speak, dress, and even worship like the Greeks.

He sent his soldiers to the Jewish villages, announcing his new decree.

"You may no longer live as Jews," thundered the soldiers. "You must live as Greeks!"

Gasps escaped from the crowd.

"No more Sabbath?" cried a man, in despair.

"No circumcision?" yelled a woman, holding her newborn son.

"No more studying from our holy scrolls?" shouted a scribe, quill still in hand.

"Absolutely not!" hollered the soldier. "No more of any of your nonsense! And anyone caught performing a Jewish ritual will be put to death!"

"We'd better do as they say!" someone cried out after the soldiers had left.

"Greek customs might not be so bad," said another. "I hear the Greeks have gymnasiums. They might be fun."

"No!" shouted someone else. "We must never give up our religion!"

So while there were some Jews who obeyed the king's orders, many did not. This refusal enraged Antiochus.

He sent his officers to the Jewish towns. They set up statues of Greek gods, and ordered the townspeople to worship them. Those who refused were killed.

One day the officers entered the town of Modin. They called for Mattathias, the town leader. He was an old and respected man. If they could get Mattathias to worship an idol, they reasoned, then all the townspeople would follow.

Mattathias stepped forward.

"The king offers you his friendship," an officer told him. "Sacrifice a swine to this idol of Zeus, and he will bestow riches upon you."

But Mattathias refused. "We Jews believe in only one God, and we will never worship a piece of stone!"

"How dare you!" cried the officer, whipping out his sword. But Mattathias grabbed it and stabbed him.

"Get him!" shouted the other officers. Mattathias' five sons rushed to his side, and together they fought off the soldiers.

Mattathias held up the sword and cried, "Whoever is for God, let him come with me!" And he and his sons, and all those who chose to follow, disappeared into the hills of Judea.

The soldiers arrived in Modin in 168 B.C.E.

Mattathias' five sons were: Johanan, Simon, Judah, Eleazar, and Jonathan. Simon was known to be very smart, and Judah was very strong.

Mattathias and his sons were called Hasmoneans, because they were members of the priestly Hasmon family.

Hidden in the hills, shepherds, olive pressers, farmers, and grape growers were transformed into soldiers. They were a small group and they had only simple weapons. But Mattathias reminded them that they were fighting for their religion. And just as God had helped the Jewish people long ago, God would help them now.

So they trained and trained, and they learned to take advantage of their size. As a small group, they could sneak around easily without being caught. They also had another advantage. Having grown up in Judea, they knew the land well. They knew of hidden caves and mountain passes. But to the visiting Syrian soldiers, it was unfamiliar territory.

When Mattathias was about to die, he gathered his sons and told them to remain strong in their beliefs. He appointed his son Judah as their new leader, and Judah proved to be perfect for the task.

Judah's nickname was *Maccabee*, because of his great strength. (*Maccabee* means "hammer" in Hebrew.) After his soldiers began showing their might, they became known as Maccabees too.

FUN FACTS
Some of their weapons were farm implements, like sickles and pitchforks, which they adapted for use in war.

Knowing that a face-to-face battle with the Syrians would be risky, Judah devised a secret strategy. He and his soldiers would carry out surprise attacks, weakening the Syrian army little by little.

Finally, Judah felt his men were ready. They sneaked down the hills, and attacked an enemy camp.

This type of fighting is known as guerilla warfare.

FUN FACTS
A statue of Judah Maccabee stands at the U.S. Military Academy at West Point.

"What's happening?" shouted the confused Syrian soldiers. "Where did they come from?" No matter how hard the soldiers tried, they could not fight off the small band of Jewish rebels, so they dropped their weapons and ran.

Judah's men grabbed the weapons and returned to the hills. The next day they launched another attack, and then another. News about their victories traveled quickly. They became known as the *Maccabees*, or hammers, because they struck mighty blows. Others soon joined their ranks.

But Antiochus wasn't worried. "Our superior armies will have no difficulty destroying those pathetic peasants," he told his guards, and one by one Antiochus sent his generals and their armies to destroy the Maccabee force.

FUN FACTS
Judah captured Apollonius' sword, and fought with it for the rest of his life.

FUN FACTS
Ancient war elephants were equivalent to modern-day tanks. Dressed in armor, and weighing tons, they could withstand attacks, and crush the enemy with ease.

Apollonius was first. Eager to defeat the Maccabees, he gathered his soldiers and headed up the hills, but Judah heard of his plan and attacked, killing Apollonius and many of his men. Next came Seron, and then Gorgias, but the Maccabees defeated them too.

"Don't worry!" cried Lysias, one of the king's top generals. "I'll get rid of those pests once and for all!"

The Maccabees watched Lysias' army approach. He had the mightiest army of all. It was made up of thousands of heavily armed soldiers and huge war elephants dressed in armor. Bowmen rode atop the elephants, firing arrows down at the enemy. The Maccabees had never seen such a scary sight, but they looked to heaven for help, and they fought with all their might.

"Melt their courage and their strength," Judah cried to God. "Let us triumph over this giant army, just as David triumphed over the giant, Goliath."

And with faith and determination the Maccabees began to fight, and miraculously they began to win.

Lysias couldn't believe his eyes. He watched in horror and disbelief as his glorious army was being defeated. "From where do they get their strength?" he wondered. But he didn't want to find out. "Run for your lives!" he shouted, turning his soldiers around, and he and his army fled. The Maccabees rejoiced.

The fighting between the Maccabees and the Syrians lasted three years.

"Onward to Jerusalem!" Judah cried. "Let's take back our holy Temple!"

So with great joy and happiness, they headed for the Temple.

But when they arrived, they were horrified.

"What have they done?" the people cried. The Temple was a mess. Curtains were torn and vessels were broken. Swine's blood was spilled on the holy altar, and statues of Greek gods were everywhere. Many of the holy objects were gone, including the *menorah*—a golden candelabra, whose flames had once glowed brightly throughout the Temple.

Judah looked at the damage and then at the people. "We'd better get to work," he said.

And with that, everyone began cleaning and repairing the Temple.

They removed the idols and scrubbed the Temple floors. They repaired the curtains, and made new holy objects to replace the ones that had been ruined or stolen.

> **FUN FACTS**
> Each year in Israel, on the first night of Hanukkah, people run with torches from Modin to Jerusalem, following the route of the Maccabees.

FUN FACTS
You can see replicas of some of the Temple's holy objects at The Temple Institute in the Old City of Jerusalem.

According to the Talmud, the priests made a makeshift menorah out of seven iron spits. Eventually, they replaced it with another golden menorah.

The story of the military victory is recorded in the *First Book of Maccabees*. The miracle of the oil is recorded in the *Talmud*.

There is another story associated with Hanukkah. It is the famous story of the heroine, Judith. Through her bravery and cunning, Judith single-handedly killed an Assyrian general named Holofernes, saving Judea from an Assyrian invasion. How is this story connected to Hanukkah? Some say Judith's actions inspired Judah to fight. Others believe Judith came from the Hasmonean family. Still others believe that Judith lived during the time of the Maccabees, and helped bring about the Jewish victory.

"How did so little oil burn for so long?" asked one of them. "It must have been a miracle!"

"And how did farmers and shepherds defeat a king's army?" asked another. "That must have been a miracle too!"

"Let us create a festival to celebrate these miracles," they proclaimed, "and to celebrate the renewal of our Temple."

And that's what they did. They declared Hanukkah a holiday of joy and thanks to be celebrated for all time.

The menorah, or Hanukkiah, is placed in the window for all to see, to publicize the miracles of Hanukkah

Today Jews around the world celebrate Hanukkah, lighting menorahs all over the globe. As the flames illuminate the dark nights, we are reminded of a group of simple heroes, who, by fighting for religious freedom, brought rays of hope to their people.

On Hanukkah, in 1993, a brick was thrown through the bedroom window of a five-year-old boy living in Montana, because a drawing of a Hanukkah menorah was sketched in his window. The community was outraged at this hate crime, and as a show of support for the Jewish boy and his family, thousands of non-Jewish families hung drawings of Hanukkah menorahs in their windows.

Those flickering lights encourage each and every one of us to stand up for who we are and what we believe. They remind us to respect people of all cultures and faiths. Hanukkah's universal message is one we can all celebrate.

Activity Section

by Ann D. Koffsky

A note to kids and their parents: Many of these crafts involve materials that should only be handled with adult supervision. This includes scissors, cooking utensils, and especially candles and matches. Please exercise caution, and make this Hanukkah a happy and a safe holiday! Each activity has Hanukkah candles next to its name. The more candles pictured, the more complex the activity (1 is easiest, 3 is hardest).

HANUKKIAH

When the Maccabees rededicated the Temple, they lit the seven-branch oil menorah. Today, we remember this by lighting our own menorah also called a *Hanukkiah*. A Hanukkiah has eight branches, one for each day the menorah miraculously stayed lit long ago. The Hanukkiah also has an extra branch for the "worker candle," called a *shamash*. We use the *shamash* to light all the other candles.

A Candle Hanukkiah

A Hanukkiah can use either candles or oil.

You will need:
One 8 x10-inch ceramic tile, split lengthwise into two halves (most tile stores will split it for you)

10 ³/₈-inch zinc plated nuts
Small mosaic squares
Craft glue
Cement glue

1. Glue mosaic squares to the first tile half in any design you like: stripes, patterns, a menorah, or even the Hebrew word for Hanukkah, shown at the top of page 27.
2. Glue 9 of the nuts in a line on the second tile. The line should be closer to one side than the other.
3. Count down the line of nuts to find the fifth nut. Glue the remaining nut to the top of the fifth nut. This will be your *shamash* holder.

4. Decorate the rest of the second tile with more patterns and colors, leaving a 1¹⁄₄-inch stripe empty along the back.

5. After the glue dries, ask an adult to attach the two tiles to each other at a right angle with the cement glue.

6. Place your candles in the nuts to prepare your Hanukkiah for lighting.

An Oil Hanukkiah

Watch what happens when you mix oil and water.

You will need:
8 four-ounce glass baby food jars
1 six-ounce glass baby food jar

Olive oil
Floating wicks
Red, yellow, and blue food coloring

1. Remove the labels on all the jars. (Soaking them in warm water will make this easier.)
2. Line up the 9 jars in a row. Place the larger jar in the center, for the *shamash*.
3. Fill the 9 jars with water, leaving about a half inch of space at the very top.
4. Color the water with food coloring. See how many different colors you can make by mixing different amounts of red, yellow, and blue. (Don't use too much; a few drops are all that you'll need.)
5. Pour olive oil on top of the water in each jar, all the way to the top. What happens to the oil?
6. Add your floating wicks, and your oil Hanukkiah is ready for lighting!

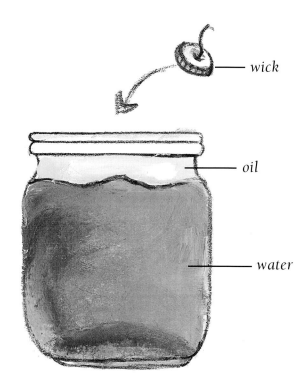

wick

oil

water

Safety Shamash Holder

This craft will provide a little more distance between your hand and the Hanukkiah flames

You will need:
A plasic clothespin
A wooden paint stirrer
Glue
Tinfoil
Markers
Glitter

1. Wrap the paint stirrer in tinfoil.
2. Glue the bottom of the clothespin to the paint stirrer on a slight angle.
3. Decorate the foil as you like with markers and glitter.
4. To use, open the clothespin, and put your shamash candle in it. Then light the shamash. Holding the bottom of the paint stirrer, use the shamash to light your menorah.

How to Light Your Hanukkiah

1. Place your Hanukkiah in a window so that it can be seen from the street.

2. Candles should be placed in the Hanukkiah from right to left. On the first night, set up one candle. On the second night, set up two candles. Set up three candles on the third night, and so on.

3. Light the *shamash* and say the following blessings. Say the third blessing on the first night only.

   Ba-ruch A-tah Ado-nai E-lo-he-nu Me-lech Ha-olam A-sher Ki-de-sha-nu Be-mitz-vo-tav Ve-tzi-va-nu Le-had-lik Ner Shel cha-nu-kah.

   Blessed are you God, king of the universe who has blessed us with his commandments, and has commanded us to light the Hanukkah lights.

Ba-ruch A-tah Ado-nai E-lo-hei-nu Me-lech Ha-olam She-a-sa Ni-sim La-avo-te-nu Ba-ya-mim Ha-hem Ba-z'man Ha-zeh.

Blessed are you God, king of the universe who made miracles for our ancestors in those days, and today.

Ba-ruch A-tah Ado-nai E-lo-he-nu Me-lech Ha-olam She-heche-ya-nu Ve-ki-ma-nu Ve-higi-a-nu Laz-man Ha-zeh.

Blessed are you God, king of the universe who has kept us alive, sustained us, and brought us to this season.

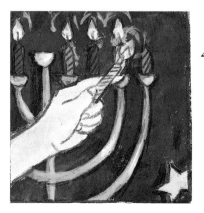

4. Use the *shamash* to light the candles from left to right. The candle for the new night is the first candle lit. Happy Hanukkah!

DREIDEL

In the days of the Hanukkah story, study of the Bible, called the Torah, was against the law. The Jews continued to learn anyway. When a Syrian soldier would come to stop them, the Jews would quickly hide their Torah, and start playing with a spinning top called a dreidel. If the soldier asked what they were doing, they would say, "We're just playing dreidel!" and avoid arrest.

Dreidels made in most of the world today have four Hebrew letters printed on them: one for each of its four sides. The letters are *Nun, Gimmel, Hey,* and *Shin.* They stand for *Nes Gadol Hayah Sham,* "A Great Miracle Happened There!" In Israel, the Shin is replaced with a Pey, so that the phrase is, *Nes Gadol Hayah Poh,* "A Great Miracle Happened <u>HERE</u>!"

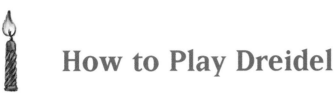

How to Play Dreidel

To play dreidel, you will need a dreidel and some Hanukkah *Gelt.* Gelt can be any small object: chocolate coins, raisins, beads, nuts, or even rocks.

Divide the gelt evenly among all the players. Then have each player put 2 pieces of gelt into the middle of your play area, called "the pot." The first player spins the dreidel.

If it lands on Nun: The spinner does nothing

If it lands on Gimmel: The spinner collects all of the pot

If it lands on Hey: The spinner collects half of the pot

If it lands on Shin: The spinner must put two more pieces of his/her own gelt into the pot

Each player takes turns spinning the dreidel, following the same rules. When the middle empties, all players put one piece of gelt into the pot to continue the game.

Gimmel

Nun

Shin

Hey

Foam Dreidel

Grab an extra Hanukkah candle from the box to make this project.

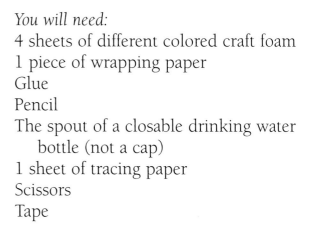

You will need:
4 sheets of different colored craft foam
1 piece of wrapping paper
Glue
Pencil
The spout of a closable drinking water bottle (not a cap)
1 sheet of tracing paper
Scissors
Tape

1. Cut out one 1½-inch square from each of the four sheets of craft foam.

2. Trace the four Hebrew letters (right) onto a sheet of tracing paper.

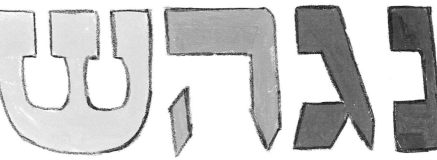

3. Tape one letter tracing to the center of each square.

4. Using a sharp pencil, push through the tracing paper to carve out the letters in craft foam. Remove the tracing paper.

5. Cut out 1-inch squares of the wrapping paper.

6. Glue the wrapping paper on the back of the foam squares, so that the color of the wrap shows through the letter.

7. Glue the edges of the foam squares together to form a cube. Be sure that the letters are in the correct order.

8. Use the cube you just made as a template and trace two more squares on the craft foam.

9. Cut out these squares.

10. Using a sharp pencil, poke a hole through the center of one square. Glue this square to the top of the cube.

11. Glue the remaining square to the bottom of the cube.

12. Push the water bottle spout into the open position, and glue it to the center of the bottom square. Let dry.

13. Break off a 2$\frac{1}{2}$-inch piece of the candle. Push it into the hole on top, hold tight, and spin!

A Paper Dreidel

A decorative dreidel that actually spins

You will need:
A colored toothpick
Glue
One blue, one red, and one yellow
serpentine streamer
A thin marker

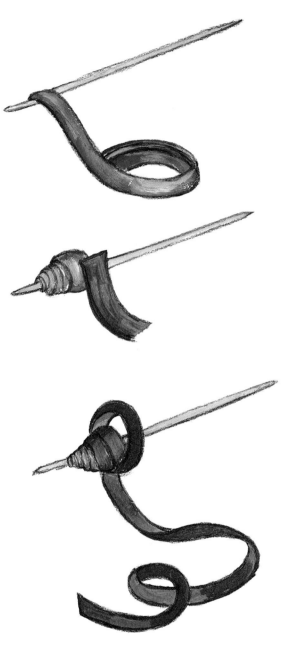

1. Cut a 20-inch strip from each streamer.
2. Glue the edge of the first streamer to the toothpick. Wait for it to dry.
3. Wrap the entire blue strip around the toothpick. Glue the end in place.
4. Place the edge of the red strip so that it partially overlaps the first streamer. Glue the edge of the red strip to the blue strip.
5. Wrap the entire red strip around, and glue in place.
6. Repeat with the yellow strip.
7. To complete the dreidel, write the letters Nun, Gimmel, Hey, and Shin around the yellow strip.

Make Your Own Gelt

Make your own gelt for playing dreidel.

You will need:
Small plastic bottle caps
Tiny objects from
   around your home

Scissors
Glue
Colored Paper

1. First, use the cap to trace a circle onto your paper.
2. Cut out the circle, and glue it to the top of the cap.
3. Draw two small triangles on the colored paper and cut them out.
4. Glue the two triangles on top of the circle to make a Jewish star (see the star on the box below).
5. Turn the cap over.
6. Choose any tiny objects from around your home: beads, acorns, nuts, buttons. Or, cut the faces from some photos of you or your family. Make sure the objects or faces are not bigger than the cap.
7. Squeeze glue inside the cap to fill it halfway.
8. Place the tiny objects or photo inside the cap.
9. Repeat to make as many pieces of gelt as you like. Let dry overnight.

Charity Gelt Toss

*If you used real coins for playing dreidel,
this is a fun game to play with your winnings.*

You will need:
Shoebox
Pencil
Scissors

Paint, paper
Real "Gelt" (coins)

1. Draw large shapes on the shoebox bottom. Try making some of them Hanukkiah shapes, like a dreidel or a frying pan.
2. Cut out the shapes to make holes in the bottom of the box.
3. Paint the box, or if it's shiny, cut out fun pictures from magazines and glue them to the box.
4. Stand the box against the wall, and take turns tossing gelt through the holes. How far away can you stand?
5. Since Hanukkah is a time for giving gifts, give the gelt that lands inside the box to your favorite charity.

FOOD

To remember the miracle of the oil, we eat foods cooked in oil such as *latkes* (potato pancakes).

Recipes

Latke Recipe

Make this delicious recipe with an adult.

You will need:
6 large potatoes, peeled
1 onion
2 eggs
3 tbsps. flour

2 tsp. salt
1/2 tsp. pepper
1/2 tsp. baking powder
3/4 cup oil

1. Grate the potatoes and onion on the fine side of a hand grater, or in a food processor. Drain excess liquid.
2. Add eggs, flour, salt, pepper, and baking powder. Mix well. Heat the 1/2 cup of oil in skillet. Lower flame and drop spoonfuls of the mixture into the skillet.
3. Fry on each side for about 5 minutes until golden brown. Turn over and fry on the other side for about 3 minutes.
4. Serve with applesauce and sour cream on the side.
5. Before you eat these yummy latkes, you can say this blessing:

"Blessed are you God, king of the world who creates fruit of the ground."

*Ba-ruch A-tah Ado-nai E-lo-he-nu Me-lech
Ha-olam Bo-ray P-ree Ha-a-dah-mah.*

> **FUN IDEA!**
> Baking holiday cookies this year? Many store-bought dreidels have raised letters or designs on their sides. After you cut out shapes from the dough, use a dreidel to stamp designs into your cookies.

A Latke Platter

Grab one more Hanukkah candle from the box to make this project.

You will need:
A Hanukkah candle
Two identical, clear
    plastic trays
    (disposable)
White craft paper
Scissors
Large sponge brush
Watercolor paint
Water

1. Trace the shape of the flat part of your tray onto the craft paper. Cut out the shape.
2. Using the candle as a pencil, draw an invisible picture on the paper.
3. Using the sponge brush and lots of water and paint, paint over the entire surface of your drawing. Your invisible picture will appear!
4. After the paint dries, paste the picture to the first tray. Then, glue the second tray on top of it.
5. Place your latkes on top, and serve!

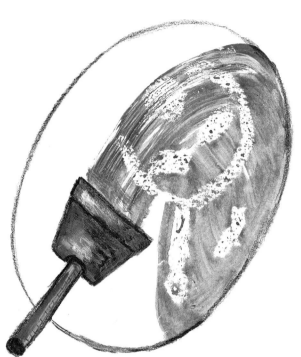

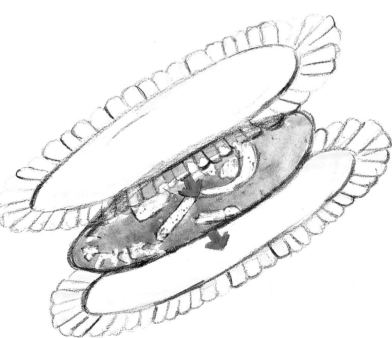

Delicious Dreidels, Munchy Menorahs

These are great for Hanukkah party platters

Dreidels:
You will need:

Marshmallows   Marshmallow fluff
Chocolate kisses   Colored toothpicks
Pretzel sticks

1. To make your first edible dreidel, take a pretzel stick, and push it through the top of the marshmallow.
2. Dip the marshmallow into the fluff. The fluff will act as a glue.
3. Attach the bottom of an unwrapped chocolate kiss to the marshmallow.

To make the second edible dreidel, just stick a toothpick into the bottom of a chocolate kiss. Keep the wrapper on, and try spinning it: it really works!

Menorahs:
You will need:

Pretzel sticks   Graham crackers
Candy corn   Whipped topping

1. Cover the surface of a graham cracker with whipped topping.
2. Break 4 pretzel sticks in half.
3. Create a menorah by lining two full pretzels along the bottom. Put the eight halves in a row, with a full pretzel stick in the middle to be the *shamash*.
4. Arrange the candy corn above the pretzels to look like flames.

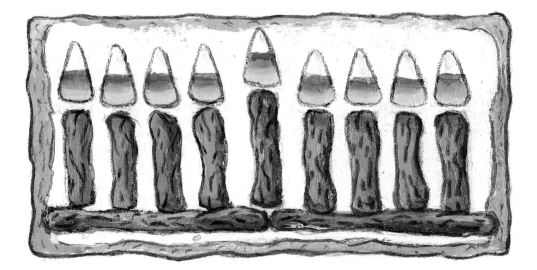

GIFTS
Wrapping Paper

Use potatoes for your latkes and for this fun wrapping paper.

You will need:
One potato
A large sheet of craft paper
A plastic knife
Tempera paints in two or more colors

1. Have an adult use a sharp knife to slice the potato in half.
2. Using the plastic knife, carve a Jewish star into the first potato half. First carve out a triangle. Then, on top of the first triangle, carve out a second triangle upside-down.
3. Carve a Jewish star into the second potato half. This time, carve out everything around the star, so that the star is the highest part of the potato.

4. Spread a large sheet of craft paper onto a washable surface. Dip a potato half into paint, and stamp on the craft paper. Try stamping rows of stars. Alternate stamps to make patterns.
5. If you want to stamp a new color, just wash off the potatoes with water, pat dry with a paper towel, and begin again.
6. After the paint has dried, wrap your Hanukkah gifts in your new personalized wrapping paper.

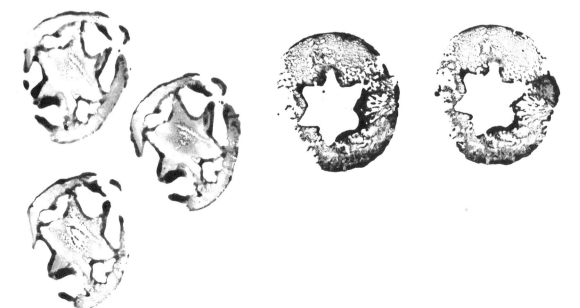

A Dreidel Candy Holder

A beautiful and delicious gift.

You will need:
One empty, clean pint
   milk carton
One plastic drinking straw
Craft glue
One 2-inch piece of pipe
   cleaner
One 10-inch long ribbon
Construction paper
Wrapping paper
Scissors
Pencil
Tracing paper

1. Glue construction paper to the sides and bottom of the milk carton. Give the carton a dreidel shape by allowing the paper to float over the space where the carton folds in.
2. Turn to page 32. Trace the four dreidel letters onto the wrapping paper, and cut them out.
3. Turn the carton upside-down.
4. Paste the letters in their correct order to the sides of the carton. Paste the *Hey* to one of the sides that does not come to a point at the bottom.
5. Cut the milk carton in half on three sides, leaving the *Nun* side intact. You should cut through the letters. When you're done, the carton should be able to hinge open and closed.
6. Using a pencil point, punch three holes into the carton. Punch the first through the center of what was the bottom of the carton. Punch the other two on the *Hey* side of the carton: one just above the cut line, and one just below the cut line.
7. Cut a 4-inch piece of your straw. Wrap the straw in wrapping paper and tape. Push about 1 inch of the straw through the hole.

8. Decorate the dreidel as you like with ribbon, glitter, or trim.

9. After all the glue has dried, fill your carton with delicious chocolate *gelt* and treats.

10. Thread the pipe cleaner through the two holes near the *Hey*. Twist them together to close your box.

11. Have a parent create a handle for the dreidel by stapling the ribbon to two opposite sides of the carton.

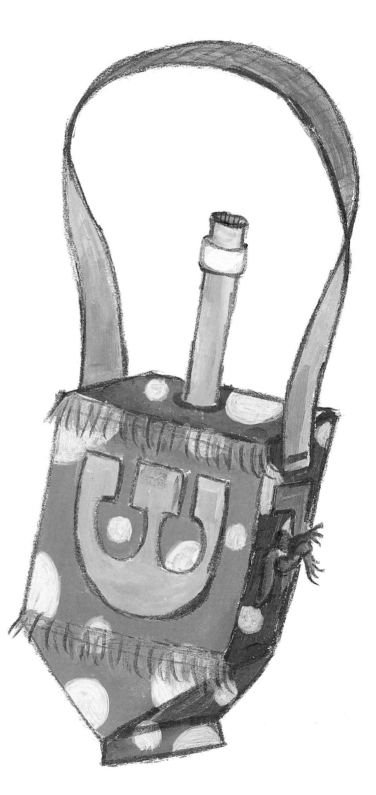

Holiday Cards

Make holiday cards for your friends of all religions.

You will need:
Construction paper
Dreidels

Tempera paint
A shoe box
Scissors

Tracing paper
Pencil

1. Trace the dreidel and dove onto the tracing paper.
2. Fold your construction paper in half.
3. Tape your tracing paper to the construction paper. Your drawing should be touching the folded side.

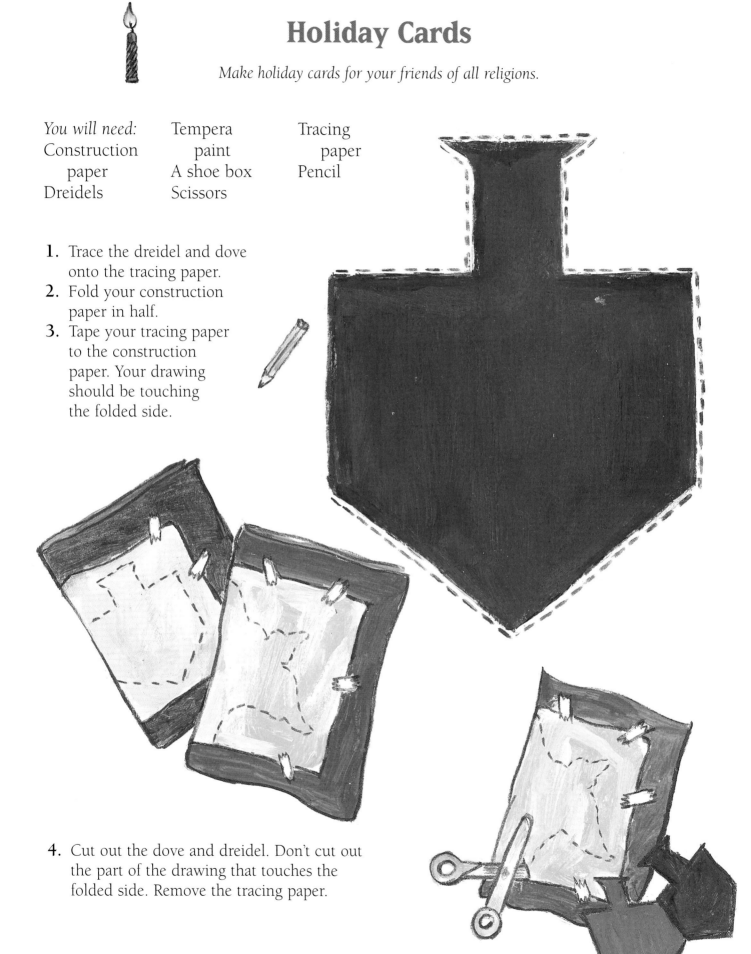

4. Cut out the dove and dreidel. Don't cut out the part of the drawing that touches the folded side. Remove the tracing paper.

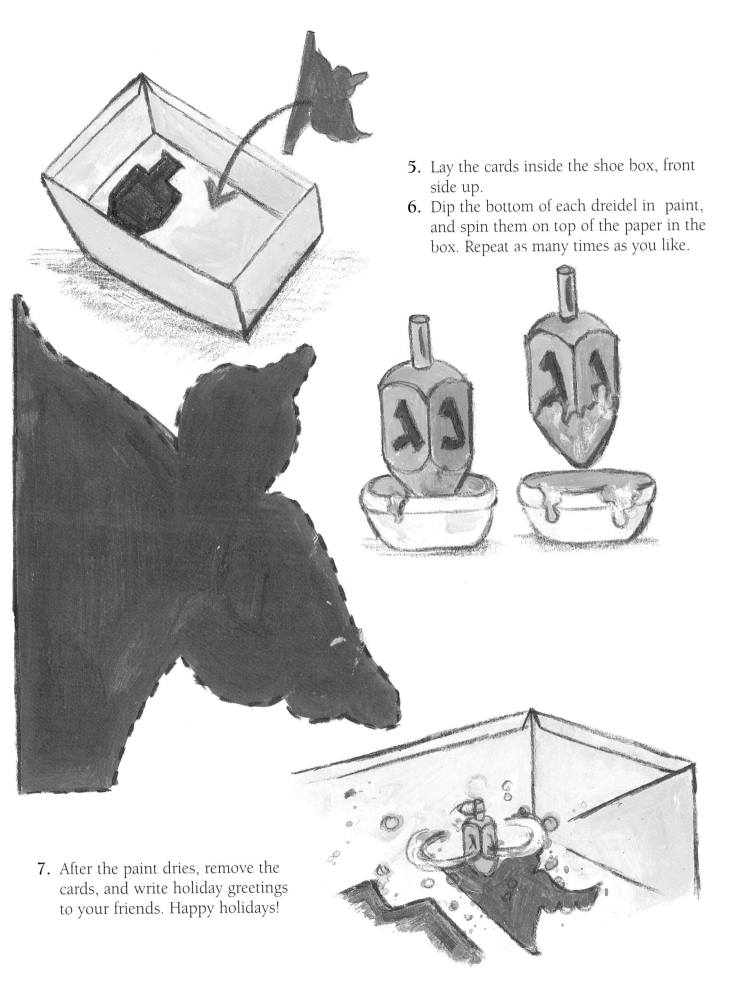

5. Lay the cards inside the shoe box, front side up.
6. Dip the bottom of each dreidel in paint, and spin them on top of the paper in the box. Repeat as many times as you like.

7. After the paint dries, remove the cards, and write holiday greetings to your friends. Happy holidays!

STORY
Shadow Puppet

Use the shamash and flashlights as light sources, and tell the story of Hanukkah with shadows.

You will need:
Scissors
Bristol paper or posterboard
Masking tape
Two coat hangers with cardboard bottoms (or dowels)
Tracing paper
Two paper fasteners

1. Trace the templates onto the tracing paper.
2. Tape the tracings to the posterboard.
3. Carefully cut the shapes out of the posterboard. Remove the tracing paper.
4. Punch holes in the indicated areas.
5. Thread the paper fastener through the holes to attach the spear arm to the Maccabee and the sword arm to the Greek soldier.
6. Have a parent take the cardboard dowel out of the coathangers.

7. Tape the dowel to the back of the posterboard figures.
8. Hang a sheet between two chairs in front of your Hanukkiah, and hold your puppets between the sheet and the Hanukkiah to put on a puppet show. If you need more light, use a flashlight or a lamp as light sources as well. See what happens to the shadows when you hold the puppets closer to and farther from the lights.
9. If you want to do more with this craft, make multiples of each puppet to create the Maccabee and Greek armies. To show the miracle of the few Maccabees over the many Greeks, remember to make more Greeks than Maccabees.

FUN IDEA!
Before you light your Hanukkiah one evening, hide that night's candles around the room. Have everyone search for them, just like the Maccabees searched for the flask of oil in the Temple.

Ancient Ads

For a fun twist on Hanukkah decorations, make up some "ancient ads" that might have been posted in Israel around the time of Hanukkah.

You will need:
Regular paper
Cold coffee or tea

Can or waterproof container
Paper towel
Black pen

1. To make the paper look like it really is from ancient times, first pour the cold tea or coffee into the container.
2. Rip one or more of the edges of the paper to make them appear jagged.
3. Slide the paper into the container. If the tea doesn't reach the top of the paper, add more water. Let it soak for about one hour.
4. Remove, and lay the paper on paper towels to dry.
5. Once the paper is dry, write your own ancient advertisements. Here are two ideas to start:

SONGS

Ma'oz Tzur

Ma-oz tzur y'shu-a-tee
L'ca na-eh l'sha-be-ah
Ti-kon bet t'fee-la-tee
V'sham to-da n'za-be-ah
L'et ta-chin mat-be-ah
Mee-tzar hamnabe-ah
Az eg-mor b'shir miz-mor
Ha-nu-kat ha-miz-be-ah

I Had a Little Dreidel

I had a little dreidel
I made it out of clay
And when it's dry and ready
Oh, dreidel I shall play
Oh dreidel, dreidel, dreidel
I made it out of clay
And when it's dry and ready
Oh, dreidel I shall play

Second verse:
I had a little latke
I made it out of clay
And when I tried to eat it
My tummy said, "Oy Vey!"
Oh latke, latke, latke
I made it out of clay
And when I tried to eat it
My tummy said, "Oy Vey!"

Oh Hanukkah!

Oh Hanukkah, Oh Hanukkah
A festival of joy
A holiday, a jolly day for every girl and boy
See the dreidel spinning all week long
Eat the sizzling latkes and sing a happy song
Tonight then
We will light them
The flickering candles in a row
We tell the wondrous story
Of God and all his glory and the Maccabees
    of long ago.

Oh Hanukkah, Oh Hanukkah
Come light the menorah
Let's have a party
We'll all dance the Horah
Gather around the table
I'll give you a treat
Sivivone* to play with, latkes to eat
And while we are playing
The candles are burning bright
One for each night, they shed their sweet light
To remind us of days long ago.

*The Hebrew word for dreidel.

FUN IDEA!
Think about what else a dreidel could be made of, and make up your own variations of the traditional song. Here are two examples:
"I had a little dreidel, I made it out of sand, and when I tried to spin it, it crumbled in my hand."
"I had a little dreidel, I made it out of rain, and when I tried to play it, it washed right down the drain."